Knitprovisation

Cilla Ramnek

Knitprovisation

70 Imaginative Projects Mixing Old with New

St. Martin's Griffin   New York

Photos copyright © 2004 by Pia Ulin

www.stmartins.com

Library of Congress Cataloging-in-Publication Data Available Upon Request

ISBN-13: 978-0-312-36294-2
ISBN-10: 0-312-36294-3

First published in Sweden under the title *Sticka & Virka* by Bokförlaget Forum in agreement with Bonnier Group Agency, Stockholm

First U.S. Edition: January 2007

10   9   8   7   6   5   4   3   2   1

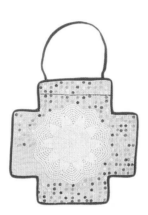

Contents

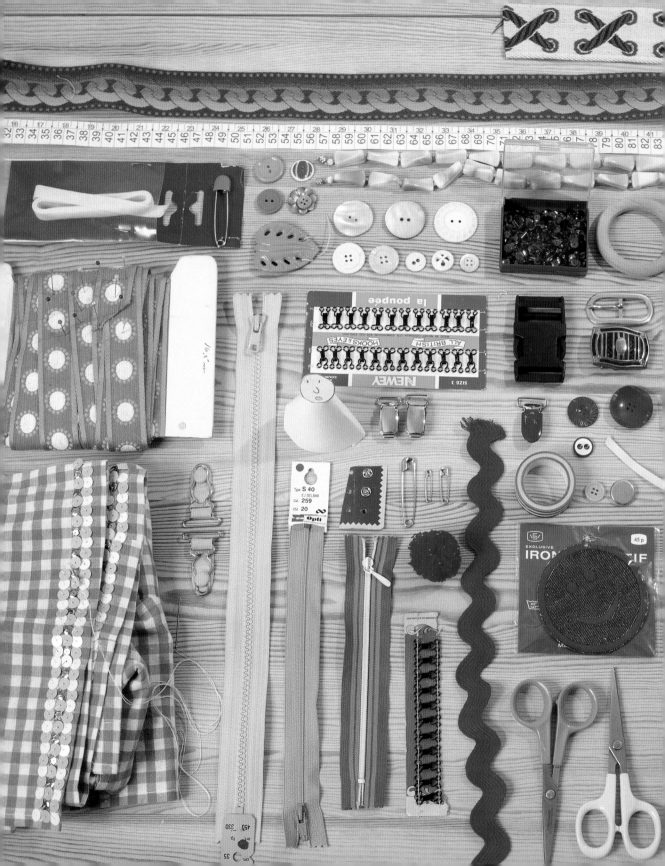

Introduction

"You've never finished a single piece of knitting in your entire life!" my mother said when I told her I was working on a book about knitting and crochet. And I have to admit, that's true. At home I've got at least three great big plastic boxes full of things I've started knitting but never finished. But now I'm going to inspire you to finish off your knitting. It's almost an ironic twist of fate. But I do believe I've found a sustainable relationship with both knitting and crochet. And I have been helped enormously by textile designers Siri Carlén and Kerstin Åström-Carlén.

First of all, I think the desire to knit or crochet is an entirely pleasant and innocent impulse. There's no reason to be too critical of the irresistible urge to buy a ball or two of yarn if you happen to be passing a yarn shop nowadays. If the two sides of your brain are arguing and the sensible side is demanding a crystal-clear answer as to what the purchase "is going to be," then the other side just has to stand its ground. Who knows? These one or two particular balls of wool could be the inspiration for a masterpiece! Honestly! And even if intellect and emotion manage to reach a compromise and you buy a knitting pattern as well, it doesn't mean you have to follow it slavishly if you don't want to. Or if you can't. This book isn't just for those of you who find it difficult to finish a piece of knitting but is also for those who don't know how to follow a pattern.

Second, I think an excellent reason to knit and crochet is the desire to make your own clothes and accessories. Perhaps you enjoy the designing more than the actual technique. Personally, I'm obsessed with color and pattern compositions. My curiosity as to how it will look if I follow a pinkish brown color with a bright yellow often completely overshadows any thoughts of the final result. You might hit on a way of achieving the maximum effect with pattern, with the minimum amount of effort. An exciting feel-ing of innovation might get you as far as producing half the front section of a sweater (that later becomes a bag or maybe a hat). Or maybe you visualize a certain kind of skirt, just like the one somebody was wearing last summer. Or maybe you find an old sweater that you put in a hot wash to felt the wool and then you make it into an identical skirt or add some crocheted pockets, maybe, or a new ruffle around the bottom.

Third, there's something relaxing about the actual process of knitting and crocheting, almost like meditation, working the yarn in a series of repetitive movements; it almost doesn't matter what it ends up as, I sometimes think. I'm sitting here and somehow measuring time, one stitch each second. Just think, this evening was 3 inches (7 cm) long. A crocheted evening is only 1.5 inches, or 3.5 cm—maybe 2 (5 cm) if you don't mind your hand hurting a little bit.

When you knit and crochet, you're creating your own fabric. You're not locked into a definite idea from the start, because the technique itself leaves the project open to improvisation as you go along. A piece of knitting becomes a kind of elastic fabric, like a pair of wide-meshed tights; a piece of crochet becomes chunkier and firmer and is more time-consuming. If I manage to keep all the rules about what's right and proper at arm's length and if I'm a little easygoing, I might even surprise my nearest and dearest one of these days and actually finish a sweater.

Lots of Colors and Patterns

Backless Top

Size: In order to get the right size, you first need to measure the required number of inches (centimeters) against your body. If you're used to knitting, you can improvise; 160–190 stitches around the body is medium size. Slightly fewer stitches if you're using thick yarn and slightly more if you're using a finer type. If you want to be more precise, it's a good idea to do a swatch. Knit 4 inches (10 cm) and count the number of stitches, then work out how many you need to end up with the right size. In this case, the top shown here has been made from an assortment of leftover pieces that had already been knitted. The pieces were pinned together on the body. The size can be varied without really altering the overall look of the piece.

The front section is knitted half in a stripe worked in stockinette stitch and half in a textured square pattern. The section with a square pattern is knitted as follows: Rows 1 and 2 start with knit 5, purl 5, and so on. Rows 3 and 4 start with purl 5, knit 5; then begin again with Row 1.

The waist is accentuated with the same yarn used for the blue-green section on the chest. You can, of course, use any yarn you like or buy a ready-made cord. However, if you would like to make the cord yourself—as it is in the picture—this is how to do it: Take approximately 1 yard (1 m) of yarn and fasten one end firmly (to a chair or something similar), then hold the other end tightly and keep twisting the yarn around and around. Then take hold of the center of the twisted yarn and fold it in half, at the same time unfastening the first end. When you let go, the yarn will twist back on itself, and all you need to do is adjust it slightly. When you have made two cords the same, they are woven, one at a time, through the front of the top where you want to mark the waistline, taking in 3 stitches at a time. Use a darning needle with a large eye. Attach a small wool pom-pom (see page 41) onto the end of each cord.

The back consists of a half-finished ribbed scarf that has been cut in half. When you have cut it into two parts, carefully unravel the row that has been cut, then knit a row to finish it off using a different color. Finally, sew the parts to the front section. Strong thread rather than yarn will make the seam neater. It's also a good idea to wrap the pieces over one another before pinning them; this produces a smoother finish. Using a lot of small, close stitches will produce excellent results.

The neckline is ribbed, knitted on a circular needle to a depth of about 4 inches (10 cm). It is then sewn to the top of the front section using thread. Thus the back is left partially bare. Knit 2, purl 2, will give a strong ribbed effect. Approximately 200 stitches using 3-ply yarn will be enough for a small size (as in the picture). For a larger size, 215–220 stitches would be appropriate.

13

If you're not afraid to change the way you think, there's a lot to be gained from a spontaneous approach to your work. On the one hand, when everything is planned in advance it's easy for that magical, surprising, creative moment to be lost. On the other hand, the more you follow those spur-of-the-moment impulses, the more careful I think you have to be in assembling the final garment.

For example, if you don't work out the exact amount of yarn you're going to need and there isn't going to be enough for the whole garment, you might decide to knit different sections using different types of yarn. In that case it is a good idea to pay particular attention when you are putting the sections together; for example, you might want to emphasize the seams by adding a strip of fabric or decorative stitching.

If you're intending to work with knitted pieces that weren't meant to work together in the first place, you can bind each seam before stitching the pieces together to make a larger item.

If you adopt a conscious approach to composition, chance impulses will be given a definite expression. You need to devote a good deal of time to the details so that the final result doesn't make a fragmented impression. And once you've found your own solutions, you can use them over and over again.

Woven Skirt
with Crocheted Ruffled Edging

The skirt is a secondhand find and was full-length to start. Cut it to the desired length, then turn up an inch (2.5 cm) or so and press lightly to mark the hem.

The ruffle is crocheted using 3 single crochet (double crochet in UK) stitches in each hole of the loosely woven fabric. If the fabric (or the knitting) is more closely woven (or knitted), then the ruffle effect will be all the greater. If you want to achieve an even more pronounced flounce, all you have to do is increase the number of stitches on the first row. Row 2 is worked with 3 double crochet (treble crochet in UK) in every third single (double in UK). The following row is worked with 3 double crochet (treble crochet in UK) in the hole that has been formed between the previous row's groups of double crochet (treble crochet in UK). The pattern looks like small fans. The ruffle can be worked to whatever length you wish.

Colors: In this skirt a different color has been used for each row. Scraps of both cotton and woolen yarn have been used to create a color palette that complements the skirt.

If you think creating a whole garment from start to finish is too demanding a project, you can just add a detail to something that's already been made. New and secondhand clothes work equally well. For example, you could crochet or knit a new pocket for an old sweater. Or add a flower to a pair of pants or, as I've done here, add a ruffle to a skirt. You can also work the ruffle separately, then sew it on afterward.

It can be very satisfying to carry on working on a garment that didn't really have a particularly individual character of its own in the beginning.

Small Round Shoulder Bag

The two small round doilies from which this bag has been made were bought in a thrift shop. Otherwise it's easy to crochet them yourself from leftover yarn. The doilies are worked loosely; each has been backed with a piece of white cotton; then they've been joined together with a red tartan band, sewn on by hand with small stitches. The opening has been left without a fastener in this case but could easily be finished off with a button and loop or a small piece of Velcro.

The cushion on the far right with the fantastic color combinations was a real bargain from a flea market. Presumably it was made in quite a random way, using leftover yarn. You can achieve a similar accidental-genius effect by closing your eyes when choosing your colors. Or study old rag rugs or other vintage household items.

The color combinations that were popular in other times are quite different from those of today and often appear bold and unexpected. Perhaps this has something to do with the fact that in many cases people were reusing cast-off items and remnants were never allowed to go to waste. Because of this, the makers had starting points that they hadn't chosen themselves, so to speak, and this might have been advantageous

for the end results. Yarn is expensive to buy these days, and it's easy to become overanxious and far too cautious when deciding on colors.

Loosely Crocheted Bag

Crochet around and around with several yarns held together, using a large crochet hook. Leave an opening wide enough for a pocket (in other words, work a number of chain stitches rather than working them into the preceding row). Afterward, crochet a pocket from the inside. Finish off when the work is of the required length—that is, when the bag feels deep enough.

Make the handles by covering a hollow plastic tube with a crocheted band stitched together along its length. Fix firmly to opposite ends of the bag with hand stitching.

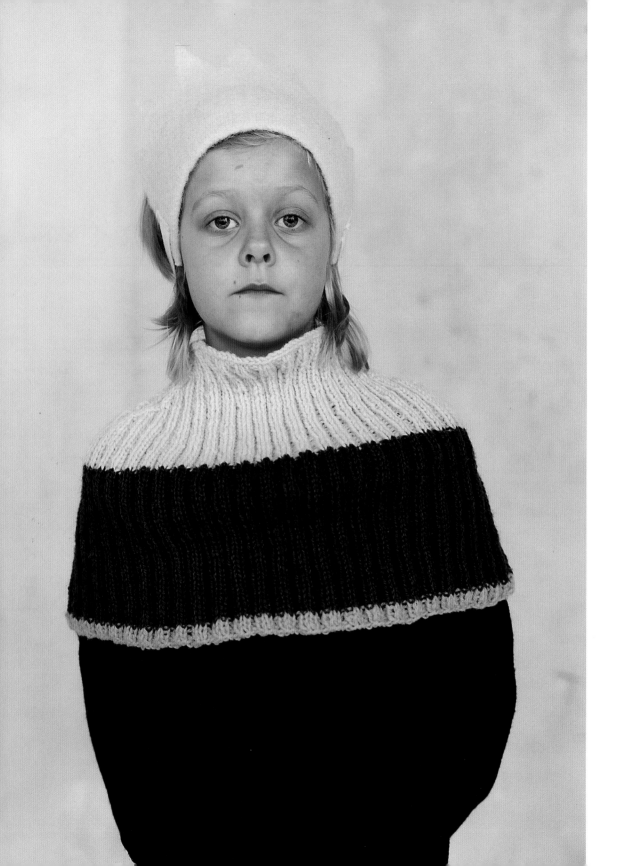

Ponchos

Small Ponchos

The striped poncho has been knitted in rib (knit 2, purl 2) using a circular needle. The number of stitches isn't particularly important, as it's stretchy. The poncho pictured here was made with 200 stitches (3-ply yarn) all the way around and would fit either a child or an adult who wears a small size. When you've knitted half the chest section, halfway to the shoulder, it's time to start decreasing. Don't decrease regularly all the way round, just at the shoulder line. It's important to measure regularly by carefully trying on the garment when you're decreasing without following a specific pattern.

When the poncho fits across the shoulders, it's time to stop decreasing and just continue knitting around until the neck reaches the required depth. It may be that the circular needle stretches the work too much at this point, in which case you need to change to four double-pointed sock needles. As the poncho is short, it works perfectly both indoors and out-; you often feel a chill just around your shoulders.

A knitted poncho or cape is a very practical item of clothing for small children sitting in their strollers. It's easy to pop round the child's shoulders if you're out in the cold for a long time and simple to slip on and off when you're constantly moving from outside in the cold to inside in the warmth. The cape could also have a hood attached with Velcro or with snaps and a zipper to be even more practical.

The small gray poncho is a secondhand bargain knitted in a variation on ribbing, knit 5, purl 1, and with a more pronounced shaping on the shoulders.

The pink-and-wine-red poncho is also a secondhand find but isn't fitted like the other two. Presumably it was initially meant to be a short skirt, but it works equally well as a poncho.

Short Sweater

A sweater consisting of just shoulders, sleeves, and a turtleneck is very easy to make if you do it like this one, knitting from the end of one sleeve across to the end of the other in a single piece. Use four double-pointed sock needles.

Decrease for the body, knit the turtleneck on ordinary needles, then continue as before with double-pointed sock needles. Study the picture and improvise. The work won't be too demanding, and the sweater will keep you warm just where you most feel the cold.

Joining Separate Items

Skirt with Potholder on the Front

This time I have turned a piece of crochet that was originally intended as a child's blanket into a skirt instead. For the back section, part of a knitted sweater that had been felted in the washing machine was used (with the waistband at the top). This gives the skirt its shape. The front was decorated with two vertical strips, finished off with a crocheted circular potholder stitched on by hand.

Sewing knitting on the sewing machine: If you use a sewing machine when assembling a garment, bear in mind that the looser the work, the larger the stitch you will need. If you use stitches that are too small on the machine, you will pull the work and the seams will stretch. You can try an inch (2.5 cm) or so at the beginning of the first seam; this also allows you to check that the tension of your thread is correct.

The best thing to do with work that has been knitted on needles larger than size 3 (3.25 mm) is sew it together by hand, using a slightly coarser cotton thread than normal, but at the same time it should be finer than the yarn the item is made of. When you are sewing an item together by hand, the stitches can never really be too small. Backstitch is good if you are dealing with a thicker piece of knitting.

Two Sweaters in One

Two existing sweaters have been sewn together to make one. A yellow patterned sweater has been cut up the middle and used as a lining for another sweater that has also been cut up the middle and then, without being turned inside out, pulled over the first one.

The sweaters are pinned together so they sit firmly, one on top of the other. A section of the chest of the outer sweater has been cut away. The yellow inner sweater that then shows through has been decorated with two miniature vintage socks. The sweaters have then been sewn to-

gether using a variety of decorative stitches and simple embroidery with beads. The middle of each sleeve has been decorated with a wide strip of woven cotton fabric.

The lower part of the sweater, which is single thickness (i.e., the outer sweater has been cut away completely from this section), has been reinforced with two potholders.

Finally, a soft woven band of fabric has been folded over the edges and stitched firmly from both front and back. A few safety pins have been added to the front for decoration.

Child's Jacket with Contrasting Sleeves

The front two sections are knitted according to the following pattern: Row 1 begins with knit 1, purl 1, and continues in this way. Row 2: knit. Row 3 begins with knit 1, purl 1, and continues in this way. Row 4: knit. And so on. To begin with, the pieces are knitted as two straight rectangles in colors of your choosing. Measure against the body to achieve the correct dimensions.

The back section begins with the same pattern as the front but then changes to a more demanding pattern. The blue and white section is knitted in stockinette stitch as follows: Rows 1, 2, and 3: white. Rows 4 and 5: alternate 2 blue, 6 white. Rows 6 and 7: alternate 6 blue, 2 white. Finally, Rows 7 and 8: Repeat Rows 4 and 5, then start again from Row 2. This section is knitted as one straight piece.

The green sleeve is knitted on double-pointed sock needles in a striped pattern. Apart from the change of color every fifth row, a ribbed horizontal pattern is added; knit 3, purl 1—follow the picture on the next page. Begin with the narrow part of the sleeve by the shoulder, which is then tripled in width because when you reach the elbow, you triple the number of stitches in just one row.

The yellow sleeve isn't homemade, but has been taken from an old Shetland sweater that at some point had been washed in water that was too hot and shrank. The cuff has been extended with a narrow crocheted band in cotton; this is crocheted right on the edge of the old sleeve in order to increase the number of stitches.

The lining is a woven cotton fabric with a yellow pattern. Pin the lining firmly to the rectangular front and back pieces. Mark the neckline and armholes with a pen. Overlock around the edges using the sewing machine, then cut out.

Making up: Stitch bias binding around all the edges. Set the sleeves in by hand using strong sewing or buttonhole thread. Lightly press the seams. Hide the seams with a narrow band taken around the corners of the neckline at the front. Press again. At the bottom of the jacket, a broad woven band has been used as decoration. Two small buttons in the corners at the front conceal the point where the different bands meet. As a fastening, four ties in the same fabric as the lining have been stitched on. Wine red pom-poms (see page 41) have been added to the ends of the band.

Careful making up is always important for the final impression, and if you're improvising, as with this jacket, it's absolutely vital. With the amount of effort put into knitting the sections, it feels like a waste of time if we're careless when it comes to sewing them together. It can sometimes be more effective to mix ready-made basic pieces with the odd small detail you have knitted yourself rather than devote yourself almost entirely to making up an attractive piece.

Thick, bulky seams never look good. When you're dealing with knitting or crochet using thicker yarn, stitch edge to edge or even wrap one over the other. The edges should be carefully pressed before being sewn together. Use a hot iron, placing a damp cloth between the iron and your work. Don't press down too hard. If the knitting or crochet is slightly loose and uneven at the edges, you can bind them using a sewing machine before you stitch them together by hand.

Deal with elasticity in the work by gently fixing the piece of knitting underneath the binding. Pin firmly with safety pins going across the binding.

Finer work should also be pressed carefully before being sewn together by hand with small stitches or using the sewing machine. Press the seams afterward as well for a perfect result.

Crocheted Skirt Made into a Dress

Begin crocheting the skirt from the bottom. Use leftover cotton yarn. Since cotton yarn isn't particularly elastic, it's easy to see when you have enough stitches to give the required width. Remember to cast on sufficient stitches to allow you to move easily when walking. Don't wrap the work too closely around your legs when measuring. Decrease 1 stitch at each side of the ruffle, approximately every 2.5 inches (6 cm), more often if you want a fuller skirt and a more pronounced shaping. Fasten off when you have reached the required length.

In this case I have continued above the waistline but not so far as to make a proper dress. An opening at the front has been created by working back and forth instead of around and around.

Circles: The skirt has been decorated with a small doily made up of circles—a beautifully made secondhand find. It isn't difficult to crochet circles, but it is time-consuming. Start with 5 stitches, and then continue to work around and around. At the start, in the center of the circle, you will need to increase more than you do as you work out toward the edges.

It's a good idea to double the number of stitches over the first 2 rows and then to increase by 1 stitch in every third stitch. A small circular piece of crochet work doesn't have to be perfect from the start; it can easily be pressed into shape with a hot iron and a damp cloth.

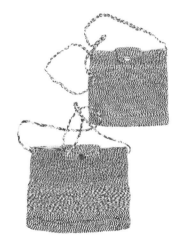

Checked Bag

This is a green-and-white-checked bag with just the front knitted in a pattern, with a change of color in every row. Because this kind of knitting is demanding, it's a good idea to come up with a solution where only part of the item is knitted in a design. In this case the back and bottom of the bag are made from a piece of tartan fabric and the lining from a different tartan. The handle is a plastic tube covered with a woven band and stitched on by hand using fine stitches. The opening of the bag is hemmed, and then two shoelaces are threaded through to draw it up.

Using knitted and woven fabric in the same item: One possibility, if you don't want to knit or crochet the whole item, is to combine the softer knitted material with woven fabric. For example, take an old shirt made of slightly stronger cotton, chop off the sleeves, shorten the body, and then add knitted sleeves and waistband. Or the other way around—knit a front and back piece and use the sleeves from a sweater made of thick cotton yarn.

When you combine knitting or crochet work with woven fabric, it's a good idea to bear in mind that the different materials should have roughly the same weight, so the item will hang evenly.

Loosely worked knitting goes best with lighter-weight fabrics and needs particular care when making up; otherwise you can easily stretch the knitted piece against the fabric too much and the end result will be wrinkled.

Press the piece of knitting and lay the fabric and the knitting on a table. When pinning the pieces together it's important to fix the knitting evenly to the fabric.

When there are strong color contrasts between the different materials, it can be difficult to avoid discoloration when the item is washed. Washing red knitting with white fabric can, for example, lead to the white fabric turning pale pink, even if you wash the item carefully by hand.

Checked Apron Skirt

Knit squares (the same size as pictured or as you wish) alternating between stockinette stitch squares and moss stitch squares. Rows 1 and 3: knit. Row 2: purl 1, knit 1, repeat across. Row 4: knit 1, purl 1, repeat across. Then stitch the squares together by hand to make a larger piece. Press the work carefully using a damp cloth and a hot iron.

Hide the seams with large cross-stitches and mark the corners with rivets. Make the edges of the apron firmer with cotton binding sewn on by hand and then press with an iron.

Finally, fix a drawstring to the top of the work to gather up the top edge. Sew a narrow cotton binding onto the top edge by machine. As decoration, a small metal heart has been attached at the waist with a safety pin.

Apron Skirt with Crocheted Border

An old piece of sample knitting has been embroidered and given a crocheted border, gathered up at the top and with the gathers hidden by a waistband of crocheted circles.

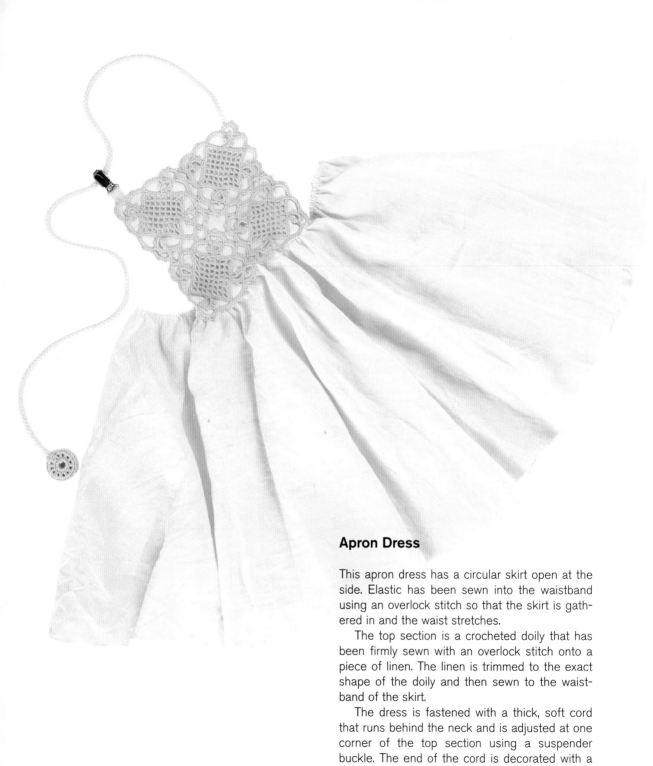

Apron Dress

This apron dress has a circular skirt open at the side. Elastic has been sewn into the waistband using an overlock stitch so that the skirt is gathered in and the waist stretches.

The top section is a crocheted doily that has been firmly sewn with an overlock stitch onto a piece of linen. The linen is trimmed to the exact shape of the doily and then sewn to the waistband of the skirt.

The dress is fastened with a thick, soft cord that runs behind the neck and is adjusted at one corner of the top section using a suspender buckle. The end of the cord is decorated with a small crocheted circle.

Paper, Plastic, and Yarn

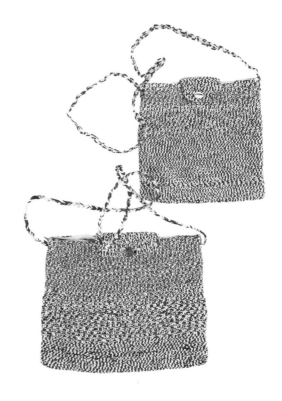

Paper Bag

Certain paper bags are of such good quality that they deserve to be used for longer than half an hour. This bag is decorated with a waxed lining paper and electrical tape in different colors (this can often be found in multipacks in large home-improvement or discount stores). The edges have been strengthened with electrical tape.

The handles, originally made of string, have been closely covered with a buttonhole stitch, using woolen yarn. Two sets of holes have been made at the upper edge of the bag and tufts of yarn threaded through.

Make these tufts by winding the yarn around your hand four times, then cutting one end in half, pushing the looped end through the hole on top and then back through the lower hole from the back. Pull the "loop" through half an inch (1 cm) or so, push the opposite end of the tuft through the loop, and draw up carefully.

Plastic Bags

These shoulder bags in blue, red, and white have been crocheted in plastic. If you're lucky you can find balls of plastic strips for sale in various craft and hobby stores. The shoulder strap is made from a long crocheted strip of chain stitches.

You can experiment with crochet using all kinds of materials, such as hemp string, matte or shiny gift ribbon, and thin electrical cable. Instead of making items of clothing, you can crochet little doilies, baskets, or bowls, to give just a few examples.

Red Bag

This hand-stitched red bag is a secondhand find. It consists of square postcards that have been cut out and sewn together with red yarn. The handle is attached using buttonhole stitch with fringed tufts at each end.

Figure Bag

This is a little crocheted figure with an opening at the front in the center (can be fastened with Velcro). The arms and legs are worked as cylinders, working around and around, and then attached to the crocheted body that has first been stuffed. The doll's face can be bought in craft stores. You could also use the head of an old doll.

You can attach tufts of wool fringe to the hem of a skirt or sweater, or to the edges of a jacket. They can also be dotted over the surface of an item, or placed very close together, for example on a cushion. Different colors and yarn thicknesses can be mixed in the same tuft, and the thickness and length of the yarn can also be varied to achieve different effects.

Buttonhole stitch: Make by taking a needle through a loop held at right angles along the bottom of a vertical stitch. This then forms the next stitch.

Crocheted Bands

A Cardboard Box Becomes a Bag

Here a cardboard detergent box has been painted and decorated; then a crocheted cotton band has been attached firmly to the sides of the box to form a handle. The bag may not be suitable for carrying heavier items but is very decorative and individual in its expression.

Crochet is often more time-consuming than knitting, and if, on top of that, you prefer to work with fine yarn, then a belt can easily be a big enough project. Endless variations are possible. You can crochet long, narrow bands that can be wound several times around the waist or hips or a broader strip that is divided at the ends into long cords that can be knotted. You can sew crocheted pieces together and then add a lining and finish it off with, for example, a traditional belt buckle.

Crocheted bands can also be used to add detail to a larger piece, such as the waistband of an apron, the shoulder straps of a vest or dress made of fabric, or the handle of a bag. Or what about crocheted suspenders?

Pom-poms: Usually they are one of the first things children can learn to make. Cut out two circles from cardboard, then cut a smaller circle out of the centers. Wind the wool around and around the two cards, through the hole in the middle, until it's quite thick. Cut through the yarn between the two circles, take a 6-inch (15 cm) length of yarn and use it to pull together the strands in the inner circle, pull tight, and knot it. Pull off the cardboard circles, fluff out the pom-pom, and then clip it to the desired size with a pair of scissors.

Buttoning and fastening: When it comes to ideas for buttoning and fastening items of clothing and bags, the possibilities are endless. Books on craft and design, as well as fashion magazines, can be sources of inspiration.

Bags that are not going to carry heavy items can be buttoned like clothes, and an item of clothing can be fastened like a bag. You can work an edging with loops to use as buttonholes on a knitted garment. Or you can bind a piece of knitting with bias binding and then attach ties. You can button a cardigan or bag in the same way as you button a duffel coat and crochet the loops yourself. Another possibility is simply to have a single long band that you wind around your waist several times before knotting it.

An ordinary belt can have the ends cut off and then be stitched onto a crocheted bag. Metal key rings can be used both for a bag and for a chunky knitted jacket. If you want to use Velcro, use the kind you can stitch on rather than stick on—that kind comes off easily in the wash. For a cardigan it's sufficient to stitch small pieces of Velcro the same distance apart as you would have sewn buttons. On a knitted or crocheted cardigan you can also stitch a fastener made of fabric. Or simply fasten it with a single giant safety pin.

Key Ring

The band has been crocheted lengthwise and finished off with a pom-pom made of wool. On the other end a clasp has been attached that can be snapped onto a key ring. For the clasp, part of an old key ring has been recycled.

Brown Belt

The brown belt has been crocheted lengthwise, using cotton yarn. The white strand is allowed to run along the back of the work, bringing it in only when you wish to create the pattern. The crocheted band is then lined with a piece of fabric sewn on by hand with several bands of stitching running lengthwise across the belt. The ends of the belt allow the fabric to show; it has been folded back over the edges and stitched onto the front of the belt. A couple of hooks and eyes have been attached to each end as a fastening.

Pom-pom Belt

The pom-pom belt consists simply of a number of small but dense woolen pom-poms that have been threaded onto a length of cotton, just as you would string beads on a necklace.

Ties

Neither the light brown nor the dark brown tie is new; both have been embroidered with basting stitch in a cotton thread. The pink tie is crocheted using a finer thread and a size C/2 (2.75 mm) crochet hook. The piece was started at the wider end, casting on a number of stitches, working around and around, and gradually allowing the tie to taper. In order to find the right width, compare with an existing tie and do the same. The center section of the pink tie has a wine red crocheted scalloped edging, which gives a decorative appearance around the neck and on the knot when the tie is worn.

Felted and Embroidered Wool

Cap-Sleeved Sweater

The starting point here is a wool sweater that had been machine-washed at 140° F (60° C) and had shrunk and felted. The long sleeves had become too narrow and were chopped off into a cap-sleeve style. The embroidery on the chest was first drawn on using a marker pen and then picked out using small glass beads stitched on at evenly spaced intervals. The sleeve edges do not need to be hemmed.

Yellow and Green Bag

This bag is a vintage doily that has been drawn up into a little bag by crocheting around and around the edge and then skipping 2 stitches and crocheting into the third. The edging has been finished off by working a cord that is attached to the opposite side to form a handle.

Brooch

This is a tuft of uncombed wool fleece
decorated with beads.

Top with Embroidered Tree

The pink top on the next page was a secondhand find, and has been felted in the washing machine. This made it easy to alter the garment by cutting around the armholes, making the shoulders narrower. When wool is felted you can cut it and there is no need to overlock or hem the edges, as it will not unravel. When you are happy with the new shape, draw a tree using a fine marker. Pick out the edges of the motif using glass bugle beads, and then fill in the center with sequins with a tiny glass bead in the center of each. You can buy beads and sequins in many craft and fabric stores.

Choice of motif: If you find it difficult to draw a motif freehand, practice on paper first. Otherwise look for something suitable in a magazine or book and trace it. If you don't want a motif that actually represents an object, you can make things simple by decorating the piece with lines of stitching and squares that follow the lines of the fabric itself. Neither your sketch nor the embroidery itself needs to be absolutely accurate in order to be successful. If it's executed and finished off well, the result is always good!

Felted wool: It's the centrifugal force, not just the heat of the water that makes woolen items felt. Sweaters you've grown tired of, that are looking a bit the worse for wear, or that the moths have been at can be made reusable by putting them in a hot wash of 140° F (60° C). This causes the wool to felt, making it firmer and slightly fluffy on the surface. This makes it possible to cut into the knitting without it fraying, and it's easy to handle the knitted item just like a piece of fabric. In addition the edges do not need overlocking or hemming.

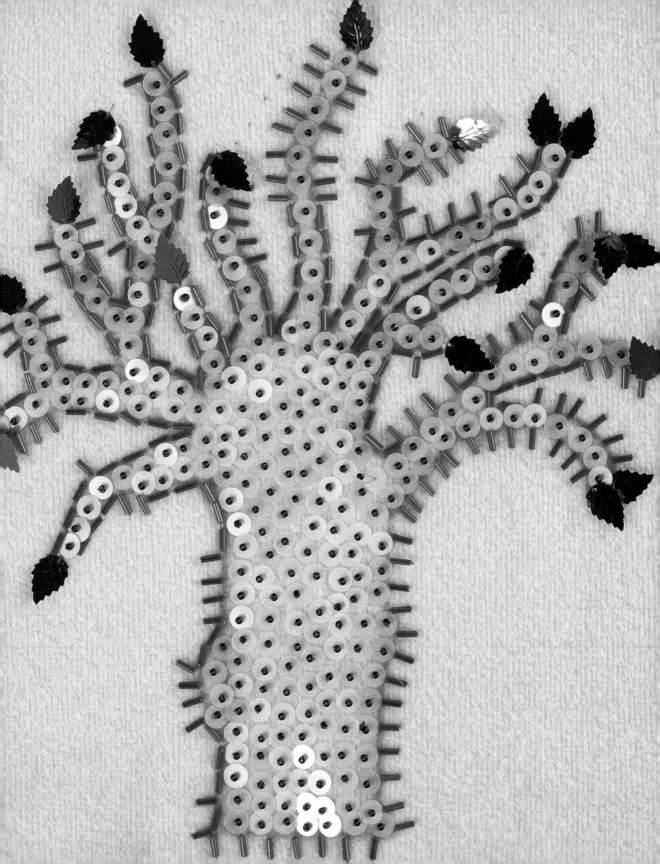

Sleeveless Top with Roses

This has been made by sewing together a sleeveless top from a piece of machine knitting that has been felted. It was then decorated with crocheted roses and leaves.

Crocheted roses: Cast on approximately 5 stitches and make the row into a circle with a single slip stitch. Work a number of single crochet (double crochet in UK) stitches around the circle for Row 1. In Row 2 work 3 chain stitches fixed somewhere close to the middle at the back of the rose, then 3 more chain stitches attached in the same way, then 3 more attached in the same way, and so on all the way around. Row 3 is worked in the same way as Row 2. Row 4 is worked as Row 1, with single crochet (double crochet in UK) stitches worked into the chain stitches from the previous row; increase by 1 stitch every third stitch in order to flatten the rose out a little. Row 5 and Row 6 are worked as Row 2 and Row 3, keeping in mind that you need to increase the number of stitches regularly using single crochet (double crochet in UK) stitches. It's fine if the flower isn't too perfect, since roses are irregular by their very nature.

In order to make the leaves, first cast on a number of stitches to get the required length, then work back and forth, increasing by 3 stitches each time you get to the top.

As sewing notions and haberdashery items are expensive, you might want to think about cutting out zippers and pockets and cutting off buttons and even collars before getting rid of worn-out clothes.

Slippers

A pair of vintage loosely crocheted gold slippers has been decorated with handmade crocheted roses (see Sleeveless Top with Roses above).

Embroidered Vest

This vest has been made from machine-knitted pieces that were then felted in the washing machine. The embroidery on the chest was a spontaneous composition, done section by section. Short pieces of thread left over from other projects have been used up here.

Decorating: There are endless possibilities when it comes to decorating a piece of knitting or crochet. For example, you can make an older knitted sweater more attractive by embroidering part of the garment or the whole thing. If you're interested in less time-consuming embroidery, an edging or a pocket flap can be enough to create a striking effect. Or use big basting or cross-stitches over the whole sweater. Mixing different yarns works really well when it comes to both the stitching and the garment itself: cotton, wool, and man-made yarn. Old pieces of embroidery or parts of embroidered items can be reused and combined with your piece of knitting or crochet. There are lots of books that show how to work simpler embroidery stitches.

Beading: Using beads, either singly or dotted over a surface, can be very expressive. You can find glass and plastic beads in craft stores. It's also worth looking for old and new necklaces that can be taken apart. That can often be cheaper than buying the beads separately. Sequins can be bought loose or as ready-made strips. Even a very small section embroidered with beads has a strong impact. Other possibilities include strips of fabric, ready-knitted cuffs, and machine-embroidered appliqué. As a general rule, it's a good idea to look at what's available in the notions section of your local fabric store. Sometimes a single detail can be the starting point for a whole garment.

Simple Projects

Gray T-shirt

Here a small crocheted doily in the shape of a flower has been reused and stitched onto the front of an old T-shirt. A circle of sequins with beads in the center has been sewn around the flower. The hem of the T-shirt has been decorated using a simple stitch on the sewing machine and a ruffle in a printed fabric added to the sleeve edge.

Simple Sweater

First make a gauge square by knitting 20 stitches. Check how many inches (centimeters) the work measures, and then measure the circumference of the body so that you can work out the required size and adjust the number of stitches accordingly.

The front: Cast on the required number of stitches (halve the total required) and start to knit the front section. The first 10 rows are done in plain knitting (garter stitch), then continue in stockinette stitch with the exception of the first and last 6 stitches in each row, which continue in garter stitch; this is so that the edges of the knitting won't curl up and because it's easier to sew plain knitted pieces together neatly. When the work measures the desired length up to the armhole, decrease by about 2 to 3 inches (5 to 7 cm) (either is fine) on each side. Then continue as before in stockinette stitch with 6 plain (garter) stitches at each side.

Decide for yourself where the armholes should go by measuring the piece against your body or against an old sweater that has a good fit. When you get to the neckline, change back to garter stitch for 10 rows, decreasing in the center for the neck shaping. The width of the opening is also a matter of taste, and it's up to you to choose what suits you best. Finally, work the two shoulder sections in garter stitch on either side of the neck opening to the desired depth.

The back: Work the same way as the front with the exception of the neckline, which doesn't need to be scooped out quite so much.

The sleeves: On this sweater the sleeves are worked from the top (armhole) downward—not the way they're usually done, from the cuff upward. Measure the depth of the armhole, double it, and work out how many stitches you need to cast on. Work in garter stitch for 10 rows, and then continue as for the front and back in stockinette stitch with 6 stitches in garter stitch at each side. When the sleeve measures the desired length, finish off with 10 rows in garter stitch.

Making up: Weave in any loose ends, and then press the pieces gently using a hot iron and a damp cloth. Sew the back and front sections together edge to edge (sides and shoulders) by hand using buttonhole thread. Sew the sleeves up along the underarm seam, stopping about 2 to 3 inches (5 to 7 cm) from the top end (depending on how many inches you decreased to form the armholes) which is left open. Then attach this opening to the horizontal section of the armhole and the rest of the sleeve to the vertical section of the armhole.

White T-shirt

Here an oval embroidered doily with a crocheted border has been reused. The doily has been cut in half and stitched onto one side of the T-shirt using a sewing machine. In order to give the doily a new lease on life, several rows of stitching have been added using the sewing machine, criss-crossing the surface.

Pink T-shirt

A piece of embroidered knitting that had been started but not finished has been attached to the front of a T-shirt. The edges have been hidden using a band of woven ribbon, which has been left hanging loose at one corner with a pom-pom attached to the loose end.

Recycling: It's still cheap and easy to find both knitted and crocheted pieces in secondhand stores. It can be fun and stimulating to your creativity to get out there and look at what other people have thrown away. A bit of cloth or a pot-holder can unexpectedly show you a new solution that might be hard to find on your own.

Besides appliquéing ready-made items onto garments, you can easily make a toiletry bag or handbag from a crocheted doily if you line it. You could carry on knitting or crocheting somebody else's work, taking it in a new direction. Or put different pieces together to make something larger, like a small throw, for example.

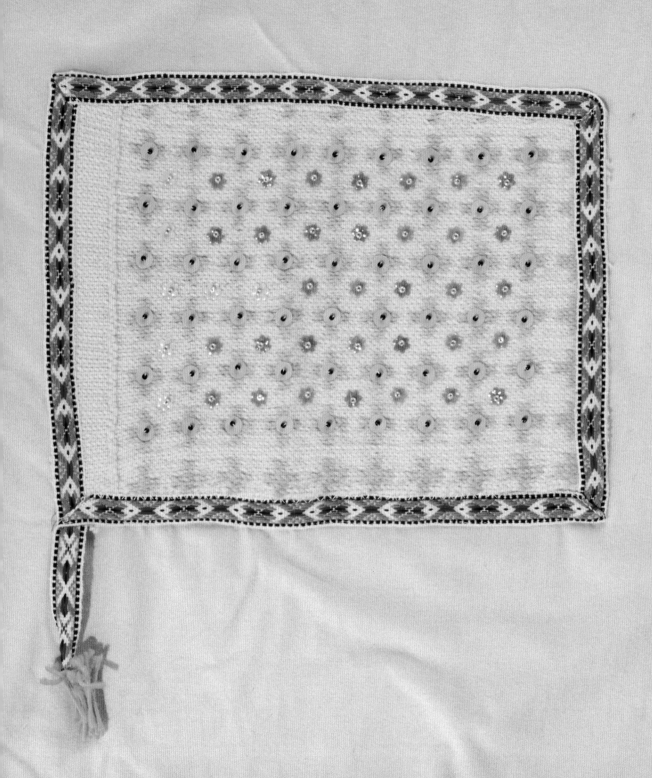

Jogging Socks with Crocheted Edging

If you use a fine thread and crochet hook it's perfectly possible to add an edging to socks. This edging has been worked directly onto the sock, not stitched on afterward.

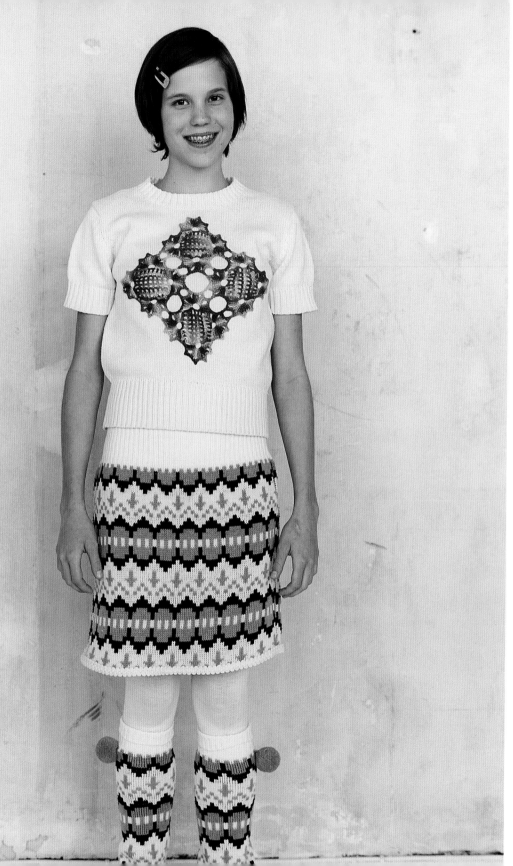

Patterned Skirt and Leg Warmers

These items have been made from a sweater that
has been cut up. The bottom of the sweater has
become the waistband of the skirt, and the hem
has been edged with chunky upholstery tape. The
same kind of tape has also been used to edge
the bottoms of the leg warmers. The cuffs of the
sweater's sleeves hold the leg warmers up. Pom-
poms have also been stitched on at the top of
each sleeve (formerly the cuff of the sweater).

Sweater

A crocheted doily has been sewn by hand onto a
ready-made sweater.

Crochet Photocopied in Color

If you have a favorite doily that you want to keep but would also like to use on an item of clothing, it's possible simply to transfer the motif onto a sweater with the help of a color photocopier.

Here a lacy yellow cloth has been transferred onto a pink woolen sweater by a photo lab, using a color photocopier. The technique requires a very high heat, which is not a problem even if the garment is made of wool. You can also do it yourself using iron-on photo transfer paper.

Inside-out Vest

Turn the vest inside out, cut off the edges, and crochet a mixed plain and scalloped edge (see page 107) around both the front opening and the armholes.

Potholders

Jeans with Pockets Made of Potholders

The pockets on an old pair of jeans have been cut off and replaced with two matching potholders as decoration. The leather brand name has also been transferred from the back of the waistband onto one of the potholders. The label was already perforated by the old stitching along the top and bottom edges, which made it easy to sew back on. Finally the jeans were chopped off at the bottom and the raw edges left unfinished, which also gives them a whole new look.

Cotton Vest with Snaps

A vest has been made using two layers of fabric, and two fairly similar crocheted potholders have been machine-stitched onto the front, one on each side.

Top with Potholder on the Front

The crocheted top is a secondhand bargain that has been decorated with a potholder right in the center front, sewn on by hand using small, fine stitches.

Sleeveless T-shirt with Stars
on the Shoulders

An inexpensive, white cotton T-shirt is finished off
with two star-shaped crocheted potholders, one
on each shoulder. Attach with safety pins first,
then sew the edges on by hand using small, close
stitches.

Cotton Vest with Crocheted Tie Closing

This is a lined vest with two matching square pot-holders stitched on the front by machine, one on each side. Instead of buttons, a tie closing has been added in a contrasting pattern and color.

Handbag with Bamboo Handles

The bag is decorated with a secondhand place-mat, cut in half and attached to both the front and back. The handles have been attached using a crocheted potholder, folded in half and sewn on by machine at the bottom. When you are adding handles it's a good idea to be very careful and use several rows of stitching to attach them, as they need to be able to bear the whole weight of the bag.

Potholders: There are loads of vintage potholders to be found in secondhand shops and at flea markets and garage sales. You can sew them together to make a blanket or a cushion cover. If you don't have many, you can dot them around on a piece of background fabric. You can use them to decorate the edge of a quilted blanket for a child or attach them to firmer fabric and make a small doily. Two potholders can be sewn together to make a toiletry bag or purse. Photocopied potholders can make a wonderful pattern on paper or transferred onto a T-shirt. Or you could just decide to collect them. . . .

Hats

Hood

This hood was a bargain from a secondhand shop and has been finished off with a fluffy lilac crocheted band around both the face and the lower edge. In recent years hats have really come into their own. Because of this, hats can now have just about any look you like; the main thing is to own one! In other words, a hat is the perfect starting point for expressing your creative instincts!

Hat with Braided Tail

A secondhand bargain is given a new lease on life with the addition of a broad green knitted band, sewn on afterward. The hat has been given added dimensions through the V-shaped opening at the back of the band and whimsical red pom-poms.

Knitted Crown

This started out a child's sweater that had been worked in a textured stitch (every other row plain knit, every other row knit 1, purl 1, knit 1, purl 1 and so on). The front and the back were knitted on a circular needle, and then felted by being washed at 140° F (60° C). When it had dried completely, the material was cut into the shape of a tall crown, just perfect for pulling down over your ears when it's cold. A wide piece of elastic at the back holds the crown together.

Child's Hat with Ears

Crochet the hat by working around in circles. In order to cast on the correct number of chain stitches, measure the hat directly against the child's head. Continue in the same way, measuring against the child at regular intervals. After a good 3 or 4 inches (8 to 10 cm), decrease sharply. When the shaping to fit the head is finished, work the long rectangular pieces that hang down over each shoulder; these are a continuation of the head section. Finally, work the small crocheted ears, which can be any shape you like and still look good. Let your imagination run free!

Hat Made from a Placemat

A placemat has been reused by crocheting a band around the bottom, working into every other stitch of the original.

Hat with Beads

Knitted with an improvised shape on double-pointed sock needles, this hat was then finished by embellishing with beads around the middle.

Crocheted Pom-pom Hat

A loosely crocheted hat with an improvised shape is decorated with synthetic pom-poms from a craft store that have been stitched around the lower edge.

Striped Hat with Pom-pom

This was meant to be a sweater to start with. A front and back, knitted on circular needles, were turned into a hat with the help of a sewing machine. A narrow beige edging was crocheted onto the lower edge of the hat and turned up and embellished with flower sequins on the inside edge. Further decoration was added to the hat, in the form of a band attached just below the embellished crochet edging. Finally, a wool pom-pom was made and added to decorate the top of the hat.

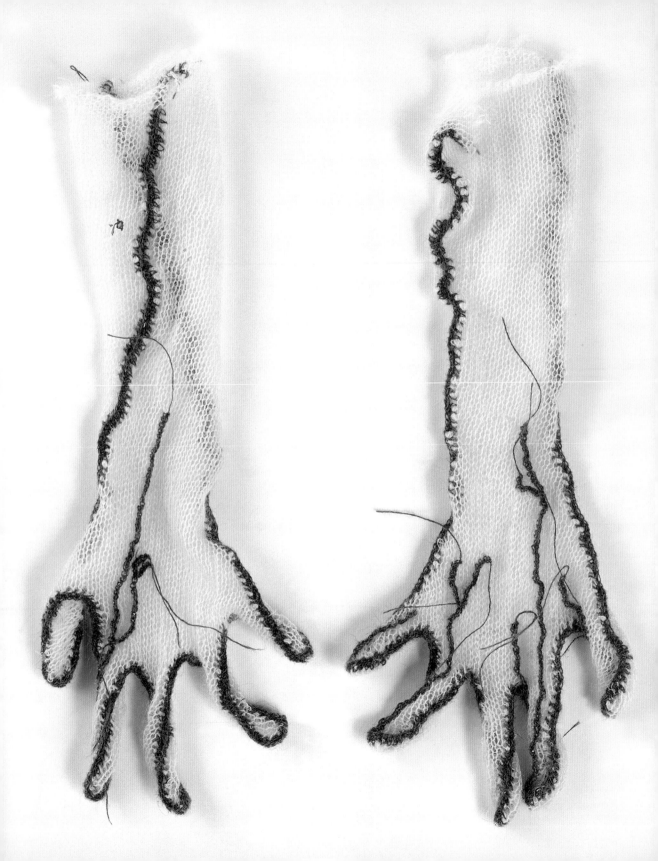

Gloves and Scarves

Gloves

Buy a piece of knitted material in a fabric store, or reuse something you already have at home.

The gloves in the picture were made from a ready-knitted material. The hand was placed on the material, the outline traced, and then the material was cut to shape. Next, the edges of each piece were carefully crocheted around, using a fine hook and crochet thread. Finally, the front and back of each glove were crocheted together, working along the edges once more with the hook and crochet thread, and the fronts were decorated with crocheted veins.

Cotton Scarf

A cotton table runner, crocheted lengthwise, is used here as a scarf.

Green Scarf

A secondhand bargain, a small table runner, has been decorated with ready-made pom-poms at one end.

Wool Scarf with Stripes Running Lengthwise

Take a long circular needle, cast on about 300 stitches, and then continue in plain knitting (garter stitch) until the scarf is wide enough. The irregular narrow stripes are perfect if you want to use up scraps of leftover wool.

Bought Scarf Customized with Your Own Personal Touches

Improvised crocheted circles have been sewn onto a plain scarf using an irregular longstitch in a contrasting color. The finished work should be pressed carefully using a damp cloth and a hot iron.

Patterned Knits

Beige Vest with Buttons

The pattern is knitted as follows: Rows 1 and 2: knit 2, purl 2, knit 2, purl 2, and so on. Rows 3 and 4: knit. Then begin again with Row 1.

The vest is for a child, and the simplest method is to knit it in one piece up to the armhole. A circular needle has been used because it's comfortable to use, but work back and forth rather than around and around.

The armholes have been improvised with the help of another child's sweater used as a model.

The neckline is V-shaped at the front. Where the back goes in, every third stitch has been decreased and that section has been knitted in ribbing, knit 1, purl 1 and so on. After this section, increase by the same number of stitches as you decreased and then continue in pattern as before.

Crocheting or knitting whole garments: If you think it's difficult to increase and decrease stitches when shaping a garment, it's easy to find a different solution. Instead of shaping the item while knitting, knit a straight piece and then cut it. The advantage of this approach is, among other things, that you don't have to try to understand complex instructions.

Worn-out or cast-off clothes that fit you well can be used as patterns. Cut them up and save them.

Baby's Vest in Moss Stitch

This tiny vest is knitted in moss stitch (cast on an even number of stitches—Row 1: knit 1, purl 1, knit 1, purl 1, and so on; Row 2: purl 1, knit 1, purl 1, knit 1, and so on) in straight pieces until the neckline, where the rounded shape has been improvised as the work progressed. The pockets have been knitted in a contrasting color and edged with binding, as has the rest of the garment. Two old metal buttons are used as decoration.

Baby Zipper-Front Onesie

In order to work out a shape for this patterned onesie (see the larger mustard yellow sample overleaf) an old onesie has been cut up and used as a pattern. The final shape is decided as the work progresses and the knitting grows. It's fine to follow the pattern approximately—you'll still end up with a good result. Sew the pieces together using small stitches, and press the seams. Finally, insert the zipper and sew it in by hand. Or start with a larger sweater and use the pattern to cut out the shapes and sew pieces together as above.

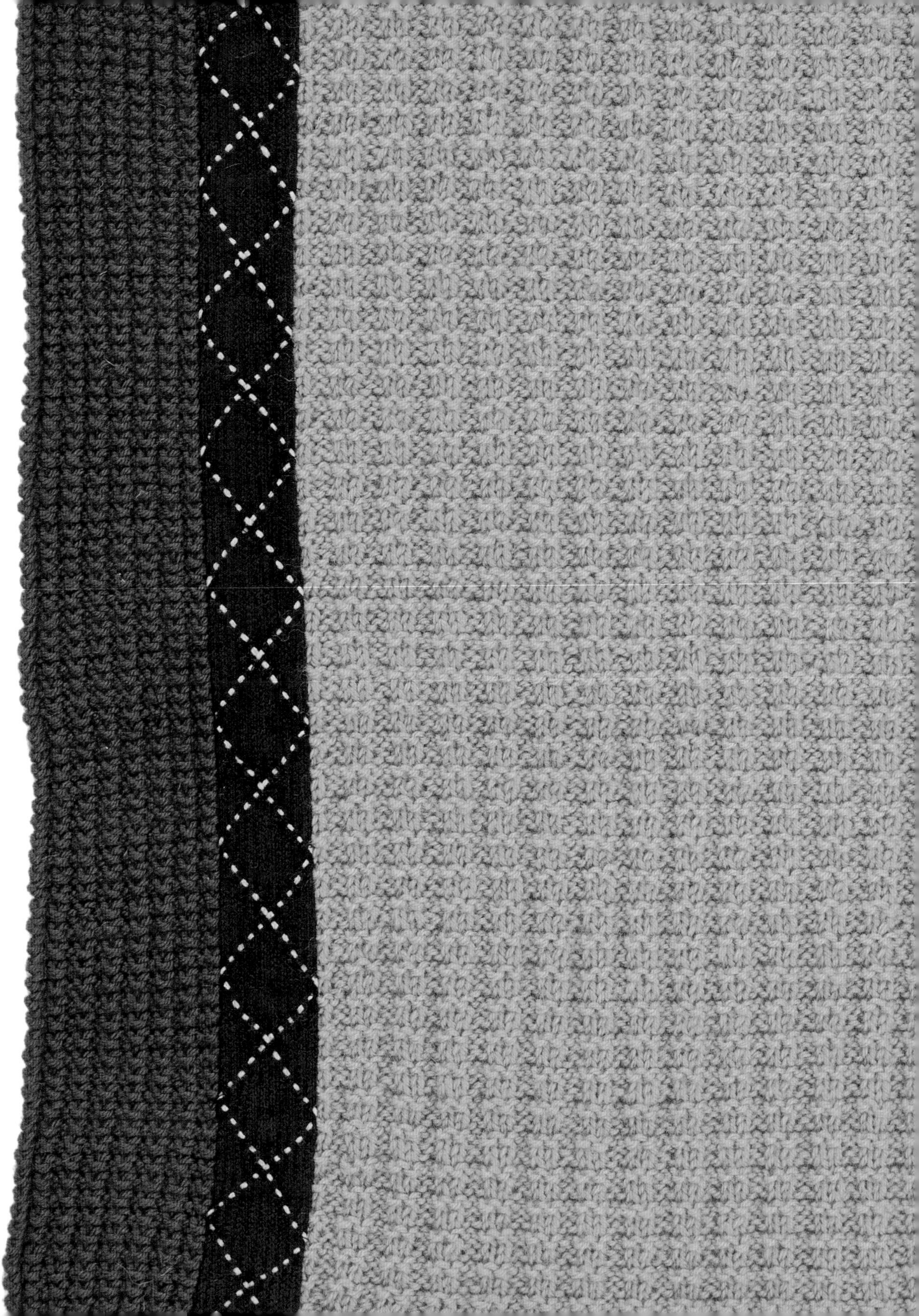

Sample Patterns

Here I have experimented with small pieces knitted in different patterns; these could perhaps form part of a larger piece at some point in the future. The section with the lattice-shaped design is patterned knitting with a change of color within each row and the pink stitches embroidered on afterward.

The piece in the middle has also been knitted but has then been edged with crocheted stitches attached to the knitted stitches running vertically, then decorated with threads running horizontally, tacked underneath the pink crocheted thread.

The knitted orange-striped piece has also been decorated afterward with crocheted vertical stitching.

The bigger piece in mustard yellow, blue, and brown is worked in two different simple textured pattern stitches. The different colors have been knitted separately, then joined together and lightly pressed. Finally, the seams were concealed with a band stitched on by hand.

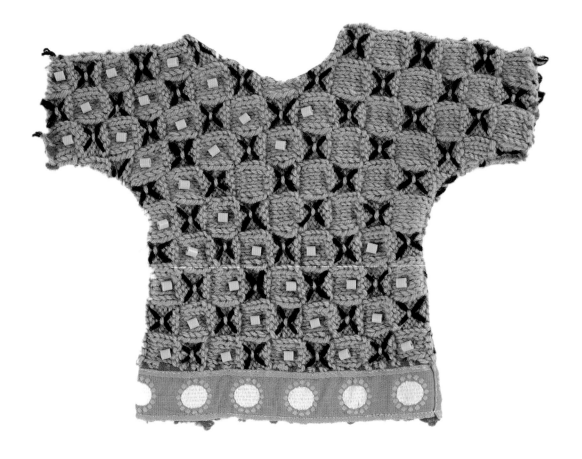

Doll's Sweater

This is a pattern-knitted and lightly embroidered piece that has been placed crosswise, overlocked, then cut into the shape of a sweater. Binding has been machine-stitched to the front and back at the neckline and waist. The embroidery consists of alternating large cross-stitches and square beads.

Dolls' clothes: Making miniature clothes can be a way of experimenting with techniques and shapes. It can also be an opportunity to use up small sample pieces, leftover bits, or unfinished work.

Doll's Vest

The lower half of the vest is patterned (see the yellow and brown samples on pages 92–93). The top part is patterned, with stripes running diagonally, worked in stockinette stitch with color changes in each row (move 1 stitch to the left in each new row). The armholes and neckline have been overlocked following lines drawn on the fabric, then cut out. The vest is fastened with a safety pin.

Patterned knitting is a rewarding technique, because it gives a varied appearance without being too demanding. For example, you can change patterns within the same garment, thus creating a striped effect. Or you might choose to have a sweater with a patterned back and front and the sleeves in stockinette stitch. Edges knitted in a pattern don't curl up as stockinette stitch does, and they also give a fuller impression.

Crocheted Doilies and Placemats

Cardigan with Swans

A favorite cardigan has been decorated with an incredible doily, with crocheted three-dimensional swans in a circle. A motif from a winter jacket has been added in the center.

It's easy to find second-hand crocheted doilies. Their composition is often amazingly complex, and there aren't many people who can crochet like this these days. Doilies aren't usually very expensive, either—all of which makes it very tempting to look for new ways of using these treasures.

Small Tote Bag

A neatly stitched little bag in a flowery fabric has a same-color lining and a clasp made from a piece of embroidery—a secondhand bargain. The handles are made from the same fabric as the rest of the bag. The front is decorated with a small crocheted doily with a flower motif layered over a larger doily.

Top

This is a vintage crocheted cotton placemat with a narrow crocheted band added all around the edges. In the same style, a band to button around the neck has been crocheted and attached to the top edge. Two equally narrow but longer bands to fasten across the back have been stitched on. The top is intended to be worn as it is or over a thin sweater or T-shirt.

Shopping Bag

This bag has been made from fabric, then decorated with another vintage crochet placemat sewn on by hand using small stitches.

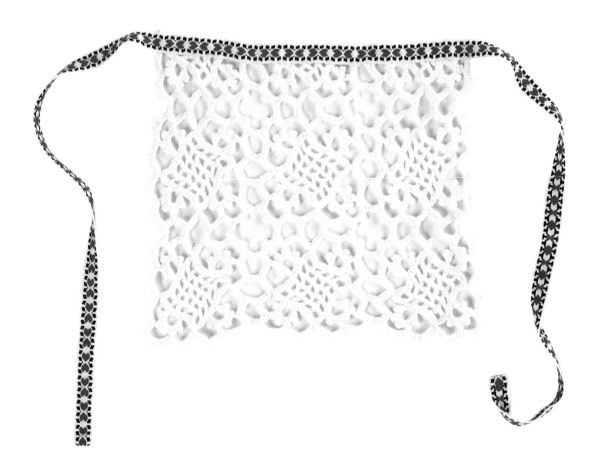

Lacy Apron Skirt

In this case a crocheted placemat has simply been cut in half to form the front of an apron skirt, then edged with a traditional-style patterned ribbon.

Shawl

A triangular shape has been carefully cut from an old, unfinished piece of work and turned into a shawl. The edges have been left as they were.

Small Lacy Jacket

An old cardigan that had lost its shape has been reused here. Mark the original garment carefully with safety pins to show where to cut. Cut and then stitch on bias binding using a sewing machine.

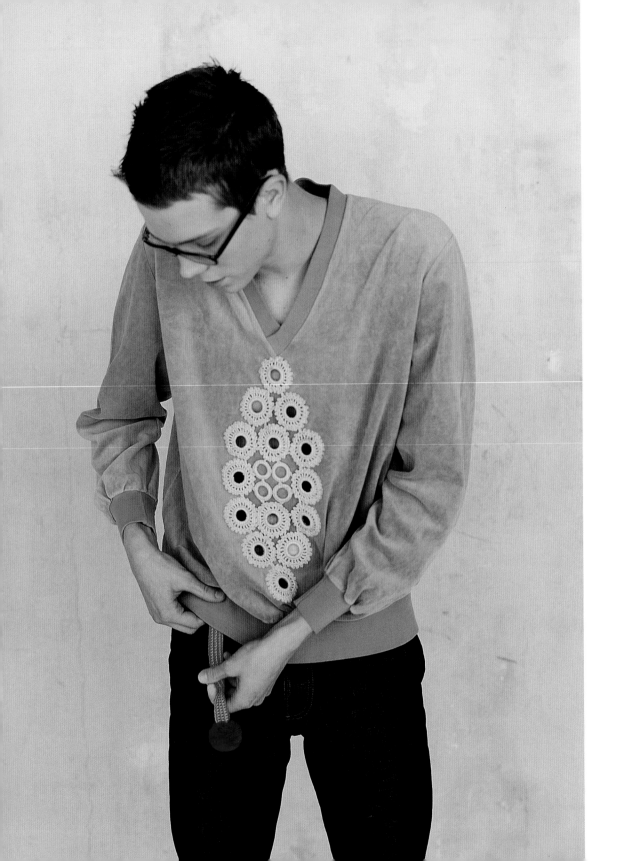

Velour Top

This man's top has been decorated with a crocheted placemat, placed diagonally on the front. It can easily be attached using fabric glue; then the fabric in the center of each circle can be cut out using a small, sharp craft knife or embroidery scissors, as here. Washing by hand is recommended so that the fabric doesn't fray.

Red and White Top

The top on the following pages is knitted on a circular needle, with color changes in every row. The armholes and neckline are worked straight. An edging has been crocheted on at the bottom edge by working 2 crochet stitches in each knitted stitch, giving the hem a wavy effect. The armholes have a crocheted scalloped edging: 5 double crochet (treble crochet in UK) in 1 stitch, skip 2 stitches, crochet 1 single crochet (double crochet in UK), skip 2 stitches, 5 double crochet (treble crochet in UK) in 1 stitch, and so on. At the neckline an old crocheted band has been attached, embroidered with beads, and sewn on by hand with neat stitches.

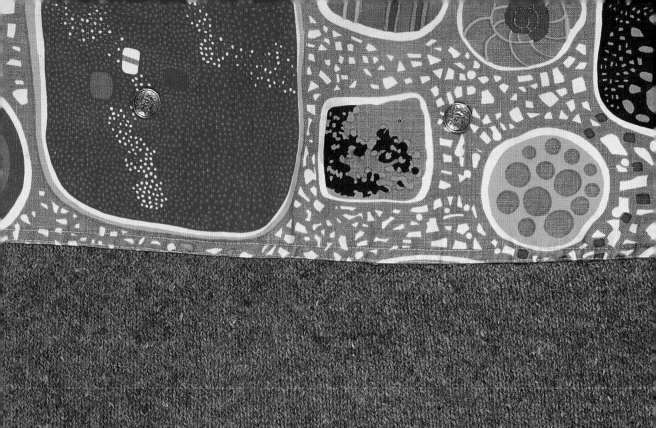

Baby Blankets

Blanket Made with Squares

Knit a number of squares in stockinette stitch and then add a narrow crocheted edging around each. Stitch the squares together by hand and work a crochet finish around the blanket. Crocheted embellishments can be added if desired.

Blanket with Fabric Lining

Knit a suitable-sized piece in stockinette stitch, then line with a stronger fabric using the sewing machine. Fold the fabric over onto the front of the blanket, and then attach using a double row of stitching on the sewing machine. Decorate with two buttons, which will also keep the knitting and the backing together.

Stripes

Striped Skirt with Red Flounce

The skirt is knitted on a circular needle, starting at the waist and working downward. It has the same number of stitches from start to finish but still has a shape because the waist section has been knitted in vertical stripes.

Vertical stripes make the material fit more closely, because the elasticity is reduced when color changes are made within a row. It might be a good idea to knit up a sample piece on the circular needle and measure it against the body. When the skirt reaches the desired length, cast off.

A pink waistband and the wide red ruffle have been crocheted on afterward. Work 3 single crochet (double crochet in UK) stitches into each knitted stitch to make the flounce wavy. It can be very effective to mix different techniques and different qualities and weights of yarn in the same piece of work. In this case the skirt is knitted using 3-ply woolen yarn and the ruffle crocheted in 2-ply synthetic yarn.

Crocheted Purses

Cast on the desired number of stitches and crochet back and forth until the piece is big enough to fold over to form a purse. Press using an iron and a damp cloth, then crochet the sides together. Velcro can be used to fasten the purse or a zipper inserted, as here.

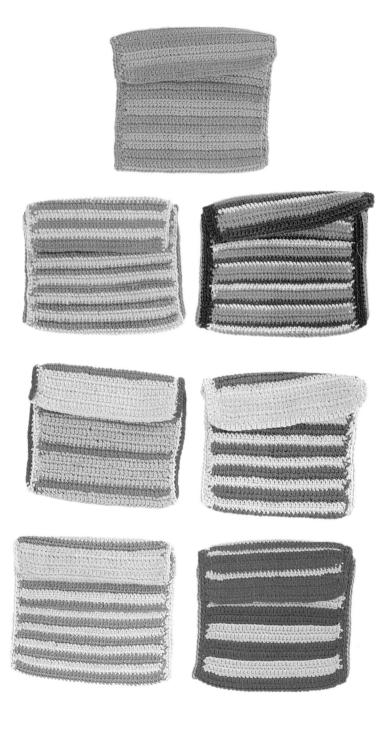

Crocheted Bags

These bags are crocheted using a larger hook and finer yarn. You can either crochet a rectangle, then fold and crochet the sides together, or crochet around and around, then stitch up the bag at the bottom. Finally, make a cord and thread it through the top of the bag to use as a drawstring.

Stripes are good in many ways: The effect of the pattern is significant, although the actual work involved is not great. You don't really need to buy new yarn; if you're going to crochet or knit in stripes, it's the perfect opportunity to use up leftover yarn. There's nothing to stop your mixing colors, quality, and thickness of yarn. A number of contrasting stripes next to one another in the same piece make a rich pattern. To create a calmer effect, use shades of the same color or just stick to one style of stripe throughout.

Crocheted Knee-Length Shorts

Because these knee-length shorts have been crocheted loosely with some give, you don't need to worry about shaping the crotch. Start at the waist and crochet whatever kind of waistband you like. In this case, the white section has been crocheted as follows: 1 double crochet (treble crochet in UK), 2 chain stitches, 1 double crochet (treble crochet in UK), 2 chain stitches and so on throughout.

Crochet around in a circle to form a cylinder, then measure the piece and at the crotch split to form two cylinders—one for each leg. These are also worked in circles. You can finish off the legs in many different ways; here the edging matches the waistband. An old pair of pants was cut up and used as a pattern.

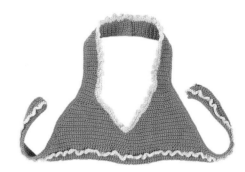

Crocheted Bikini

The measurements for the striped bikini were taken from an old bikini, cut up and used as a pattern. Start with the top, first crocheting the white band that will knot at the back. Onto this band crochet the cups, working from bottom up. After only an inch or so (a couple of centimeters), start to decrease the number of stitches at each side of each cup, until they end in a point. Then add an edging to the cups, continuing the inner edging to form the band that will become the halter neck ties.

Work the lower part in circles from the waist downward. Then continue with the back section to form the gusset that is brought up and forward. Follow the original model as closely as possible with regard to increasing and decreasing the number of stitches.

Crochet a white edging around the legs and hips. The edging around the hips is extended to form two strips that tie at the front. Finally, add horizontal stripes to the bikini by working rows of single (double crochet in UK) stitches afterward.

Top with Ruffle

Begin at the bottom by crocheting the band that will tie at the back. Then continue to work the front from the bottom upward. It doesn't separate until about 2 inches (5 cm) up. Taper the two cups gradually and symmetrically up toward the point, which should be the same width as the halter neck ties. Continue until the pieces are long enough to fasten comfortably at the back of the neck.

Make the fastening with a small crocheted loop and button. Finally, add a little ruffle by crocheting 2 stitches into each stitch all the way across the bottom band and around the neck opening.

Striped Halter Top

Begin at the bottom, working back and forth rather than in circles, so that the halter top is open at the back, where it will fasten. Work for approximately 3 inches (7 cm). This top is slightly longer than a normal bikini top and is intended for a smaller bust. Decrease to form a long, diagonal, symmetrical shape. Crochet an edging to match around the bottom and top edges ending in two cords crocheted in chain stitch for the neck ties.

Striped Tank Top

Begin at the waist and crochet straight up as far as the armholes. Every other row is made up of single crochet (double crochet in UK) only, and the alternate row is crocheted with 3 double crochet (treble crochet in UK) in 1 stitch, skip 2 stitches, 3 double crochet (treble crochet in UK) in 1 stitch, skip 2 stitches, and so on.

After the armhole, the top divides with a symmetrical decrease on each side until it measures just over an inch (2.5 cm) wide. The shoulder straps are made up of crocheted circles: start by working approximately 10 chain stitches, and then close the circle with a single stitch. Then work a number of double crochet (treble crochet in UK) stitches around the circle so that it feels solid. The top also has a crocheted scalloped edging and a crocheted rose in the center (see page 52).

Contributors

A big thank-you to the people who have helped create the following items in this book!

Kerstin Åström-Carlén
Loosely Crocheted Bag, page 16
Brown Belt, page 43
Sleeveless Top with Roses, page 52
Child's Hat with Ears, page 80
Blanket Made with Squares, page 111
Crocheted Purses, page 114
Crocheted Bags, page 117

Kerstin Åström-Carlén and Cilla Ramnek
Pom-pom Belt, page 43
Embroidered Vest, page 55

Siri Carlén
Figure Bag, page 39
Sleeveless Top with Roses, page 52
Inside-out Vest, page 69
Hat with Beads, page 81
Gloves, page 85
Bought Scarf Customized with Your Own Personal Touches, page 87
Crocheted Knee-Length Shorts, page 117
Crocheted Bikini, page 121
Top with Ruffle, page 121
Striped Halter Top, page 122

Hugo Carlén
Ties, page 44

Karin Södergren
Brooch, page 48